LET'S DRAW BUGS AND CRITTERS WITH CRAYOLA!

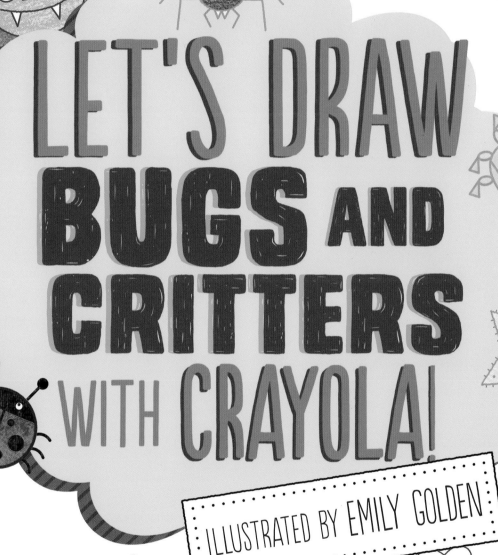

ILLUSTRATED BY EMILY GOLDEN

LERNER PUBLICATIONS ◆ MINNEAPOLIS

© 2019 Crayola, Easton, PA 18044-0431. Crayola Oval Logo, Crayola, Serpentine Design, Carnation Pink, Tickle Me Pink, Pink Flamingo, Banana Mania, Inchworm, and Granny Smith Apple are registered trademarks of Crayola used under license.

Official Licensed Product
Lerner Publications Company
A division of Lerner Publishing Group, Inc.
241 First Avenue North
Minneapolis, MN 55401 USA

For reading levels and more information, look up this title at www.lernerbooks.com.

Main body text set in Billy Infant Regular 24/30.
Typeface provided by SparkyType.

Library of Congress Cataloging-in-Publication Data

Names: Golden, Emily (Illustrator), illustrator.
Title: Let's draw bugs and critters with Crayola! / illustrated by Emily Golden.
Description: Minneapolis : Lerner Publications, 2019. | Series: Let's draw with Crayola! | Includes bibliographical references. | Audience: Ages 4-9. | Audience: K to Grade 3.
Identifiers: LCCN 2017061822 (print) | LCCN 2017060896 (ebook) | ISBN 9781541512535 (eb pdf) | ISBN 9781541511019 (lb : alk. paper)
Subjects: LCSH: Animals in art—Juvenile literature. | Insects in art—Juvenile literature. | Drawing—Technique—Juvenile literature.
Classification: LCC NC780 (print) | LCC NC780 .L426 2019 (ebook) | DDC 743.6/57—dc23

LC record available at https://lccn.loc.gov/2017061822

Manufactured in the United States of America
1-43985-33999-6/21/2018

CONTENTS

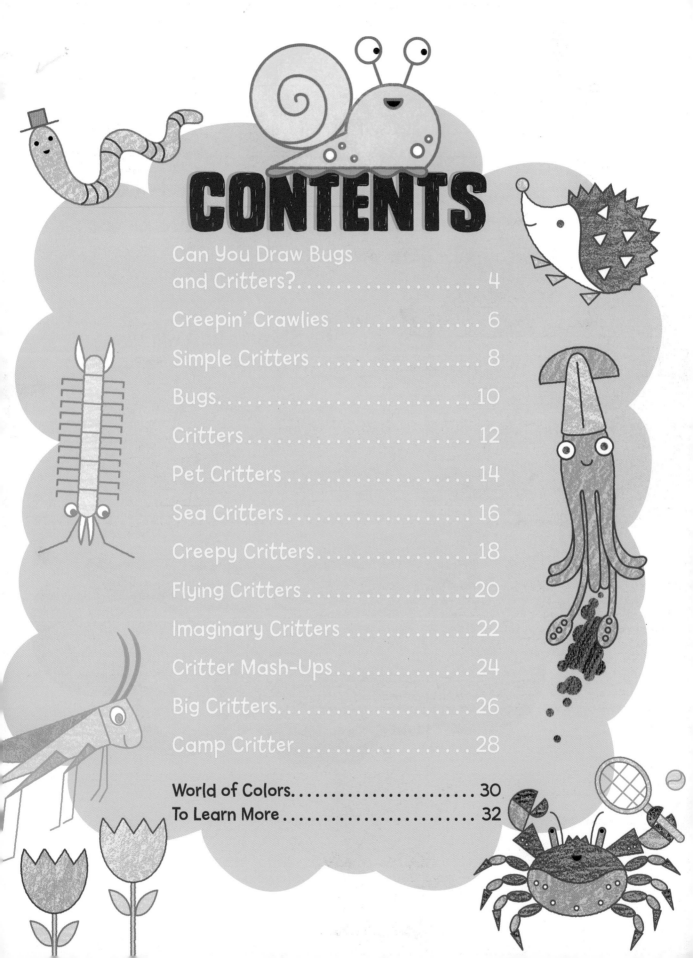

CAN YOU DRAW BUGS AND CRITTERS?

You can if you can draw shapes! Use the shapes in the box at the top of each page to draw the bug or critter parts. Put the parts together in your drawing to make a slithering snake or a squeaky mouse. Or use the parts to make your own critter!

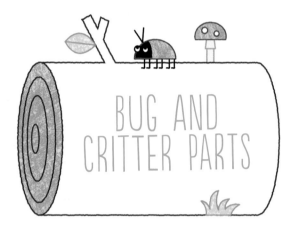

BUG AND CRITTER PARTS

Shapes you will use:

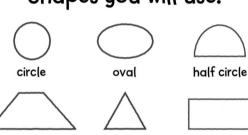

circle oval half circle

trapezoid triangle rectangle

Wings

Eyes

Paws and Claws

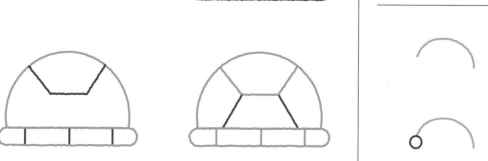

Shell and Antennae

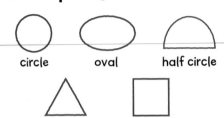
Pinky

Spot

Anton

Brian

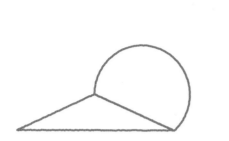 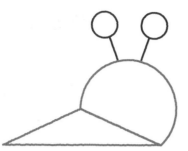 

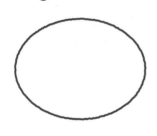 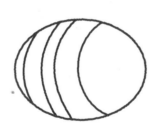 

Honey

Shapes you will use:

 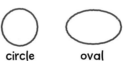

circle   oval   half circle   triangle

Tweet

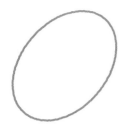  

Cheddar

  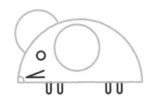 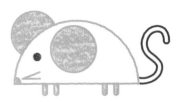

Moley

 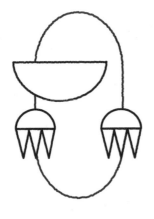  

8

Spike

Bubbles

9

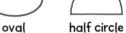

Flutter

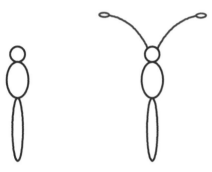

10

Buzz

Hopper

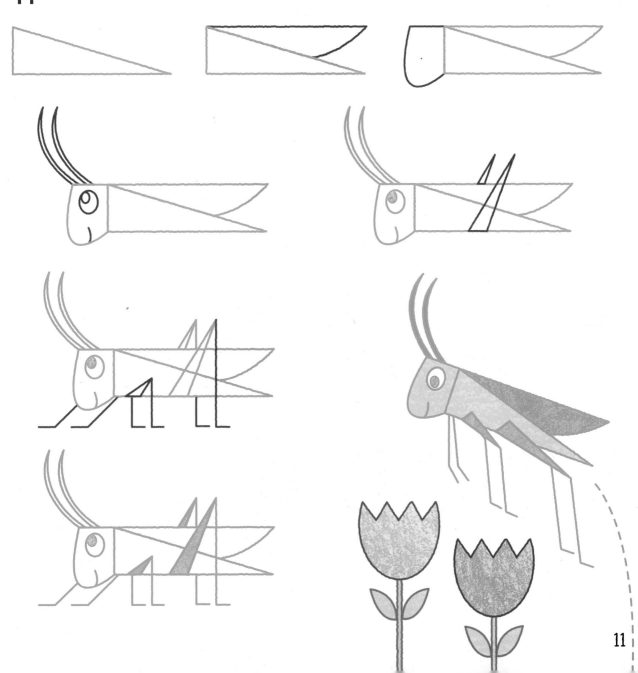

CRITTERS

Burt

Tiny

12

Cheeks

Critter House

PET CRITTERS

Herman

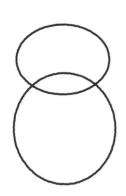   

Shelly

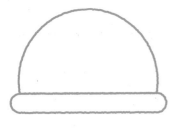 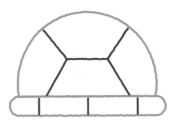 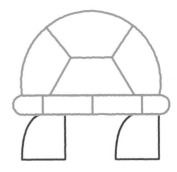

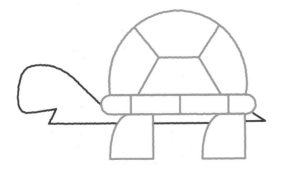 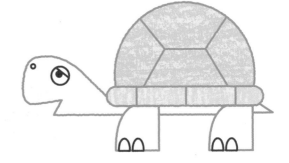

Slither

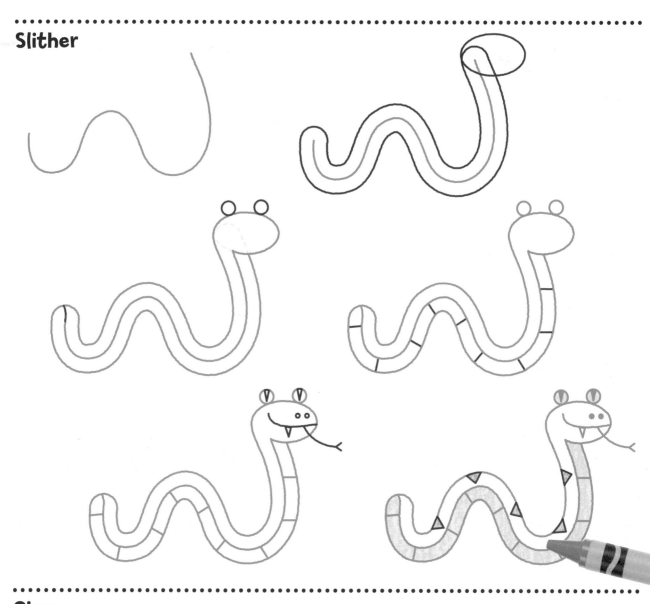

Gizmo

Shapes you will use:

circle   oval   half circle

trapezoid   triangle

Una the Urchin

Inky

Oops!

Star

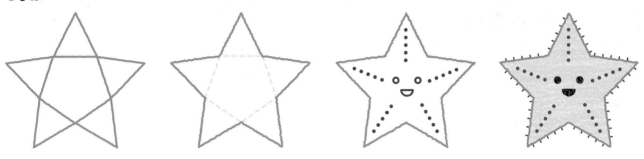

Pincer

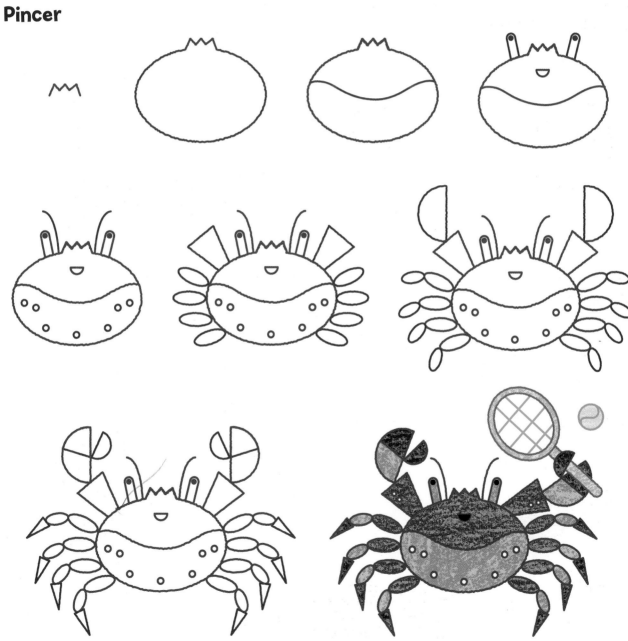

CREEPY CRITTERS

Silky

Tarantula

18

Centipete

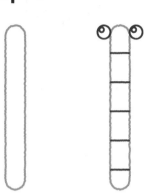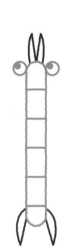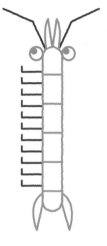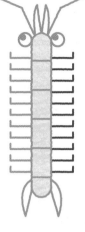

Moonlight

19

Shapes you will use:

circle   oval   half circle   triangle

Firefly

Screech

Sky

Rainbow

IMAGINARY CRITTERS

Lovebug

Leafy

Binocular bug

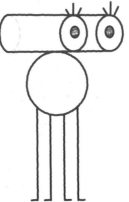

Hairy Harry

CRITTER MASH-UPS

Shapes you will use:

circle oval half circle

triangle rectangle

Bunnyfly

24

Bugbear

Foxdeer

25

BIG CRITTERS

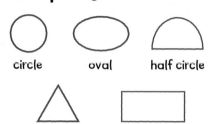
The Capybara

26

Smokey

FINISH

WORLD OF COLORS

The world is full of colors! Here are some of the Crayola® crayon colors used in this book. What colors will you use to draw your next critter?

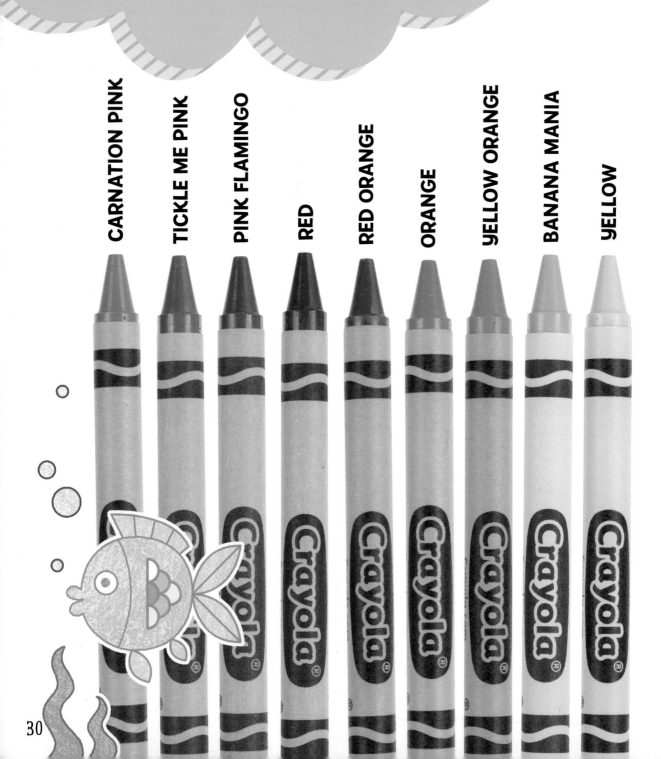

CARNATION PINK

TICKLE ME PINK

PINK FLAMINGO

RED

RED ORANGE

ORANGE

YELLOW ORANGE

BANANA MANIA

YELLOW

GO NUTS!
GO DRAW!

INCHWORM
FERN
GRANNY SMITH APPLE
GREEN
ROBIN'S EGG BLUE
TURQUOISE BLUE
NAVY BLUE
BLUE VIOLET
VIOLET

TO LEARN MORE

Books

Bergin, Mark. *It's Fun to Draw Creepy-Crawlies.* New York: Sky Pony, 2015.
Follow the step-by-step instructions in this book to learn how to draw other critters and creepy-crawlies.

Learn to Draw Birds & Butterflies: Step-By-Step Instructions for More Than 25 Winged Creatures. Illustrated by Robbin Cuddy. Lake Forest, CA: Walter Foster, 2016.
Check out this book to draw birds, butterflies, and other critters that have wings.

Let's Draw Animals with Crayola! Illustrated by Ana Bermejo. Minneapolis: Lerner Publications, 2018.
Learn how to draw other critters and animals in this fun book.

Websites

Book on a Stick
http://www.crayola.com/crafts/book-on-a-stick-craft/
Follow the steps to create your own buggy book. Then use your drawing skills to illustrate some bugs and critters in the book!

How to Draw Insects
https://www.artforkidshub.com/how-to-draw/animals/insects/
Visit this website to learn how to draw other bugs and insects.